How to Study SMARTER! NOT Harder!

Effective Smart study tips and techniques to study in half the time!

Shahana S.

Copyright © 2020 Shahana S.

All rights reserved. No part of this book may be reproduced, distributed, or transmitted in any form or by any means, including photocopying, recording, or other electronic or mechanical methods, without the prior written permission of the author, except in the case of brief quotations embodied in critical reviews and certain other noncommercial uses permitted by copyright law.

Contents

1. Smart study vs. hard study
2. Hard Study Myth
3. Smart Study Fact
4. How to use this book
5. Decoding your study
6. Self-evaluation - #1 Technique
7. Spaced repetition - #2 Technique
8. Random Problem - #3 Technique
9. S3QR - #4 Technique
10. Mnemonics - #5 Technique
11. Motive to Study
12. One last thing!

1
Smart Study vs Hard Study

Do you spend hours every day studying?
Yet, you can't recall what you have studied?

Does it happen to you that you're well prepared for an exam and when you enter the exam room, you go Blank!?
You forget everything!

You get confused for every question,
and no matter how hard you try,
you are unable to recall what you have studied?!
And your results are not as promising as you have anticipated??!

Despite spending hours of study every day, you can't recall what you have studied?
You begin to question if it was all a waste?

Every effort you did, DIDN'T Help You succeed?

You begin to doubt yourself.
"What did I miss"?
"What did I do wrong"?
"Why didn't it work for ME!"?

You are not alone!

Many of the students feel the same way.
The problem is not YOU.
It's never You!
It's the way you study!

The way you study has a significant impact on how well you can perform in any subject.

The fact is every student has the potential to excel.

The only difference is how practical is their study strategy!

By just changing the way you study, you can dramatically improve your efficiency.

The **SMART STUDY Techniques** is all about how you can study
Effective,
Efficient, and
SMART!

2
Study Hard Myths

Since childhood, we have been told time again and again that to excel in academics, we need to study hard.

But how do we study?

Well, the golden rule followed is rereading text again and again until it is burned into the memory! And of course, you need to study for long hours every day!
I'm sure many of you do that. I sure did!
(guilty)

Most of the students around the world practice these strategies.
Long hours of study- Cramming- reciting and writing or what we call rote learning.

Myth – Studying long hours is the most efficient study.

While all these strategies make you feel productive and make you believe you have mastered your "subjects."
All these never really work!

Why?
Because to gain true mastery and durability of what you study, you need to be able to retain what you study.
Also, recall it when you need it!
and these approaches? It never seems to work.
They are just a waste of your time and energy!

Studying hard makes you look like you're studying a lot!

But, in reality, nothing is going in.
You're just feeding your brain some information that is not getting processed!

The Hard Study Habits;
Many students usually stick to one technique and one technique alone.
Which they believe works best for them.

They end up using it for years and don't want to change it and will be too frightened to try out new methods.

They feel that any new method which finishes their study quickly and easily doesn't prepare them well for the exam.

They get used to working so hard every time that they feel they haven't studied if they're able to finish it in half the time.
For them, the hard study is a habit that should not be messed with.

Study while making notes technique-
Well, it's good to make notes, but just copy-pasting the same context is not an effective way.

3
Smart Study

168.
That's the number of hours we have in a week.

If you're a student, you probably feel like this isn't enough.
It doesn't matter if you study for 6 hours or 8 hours every day.
When it comes to effective study strategy, it's not the number of hours you study, it's the right strategy you use!
This is what Smart Study is all about.

Differentiating between a Genius and an average person is, they are better learners.

So what exactly is a Smart Study? And how do we do it?

The key purpose of a Smart Study is to be involved in an **Active Study**.

An Active Study is the ability to _Understand, Retain, and Recall the concepts._ - **U2R**

A Study is said to be an effective study when you're able to - U2R
- U - **Understand** what you study;
    - To know the key idea of the topics/ concepts.
    - Able to differentiate between the concepts.

- R - Able to **Retain** what you study;
    - Remember what you have studied longer.
    - Without missing key information.

- R - Able to **Recall** what you studied;
    - Remember the information clearly.
    - Without any confusion and in any environment settings.

Unlike cramming, during a smart study, you can process information efficiently and effectively!
This helps you to study better and be more productive, even if it is for just a few hours.

Cram study - it's like writing in sand, today you know, tomorrow it's gone.

4
How to use this Book

First of all, thank you for purchasing this book!
I understand studies can be overwhelming.
You can get lazy, distracted, and demotivated.
So, I am not gonna bore you with my words.
I know most of you don't have the patience to read the book completely and some of you may read it cover to cover.
Either way, this book is designed to be used in 2 ways.

1 - The Bookworm reader;
You can read this book to the end. This will help you understand the concepts better.
2 - The Skim and skip reader;
At the end of each chapter, all the key points are summarised so you can refer to them.

I suggest you read this book once and use the key summary points from time to time for a glance whenever you need them.

Now I don't expect you to implement everything given in this book all at once. You can start small. Pick a topic and go through the technicals given in this book, analyze which technique will be best to use for the given topic.

5
Decoding Your Study

The key to studying any subject effectively is your study approach!
But, a lot of students make the mistake of using the same study technique for every subject.

Pre-planning and Analysis:
Analyzing and planning your study this will be your first step.

So, before you begin your study, you must analyze your subjects and topics.
By knowing what to study and how much to study helps you in devising your study plans and also, helps you identify which smart study techniques to use.

For example,

If you are preparing for a test, there is no point to study 'cover to cover' of your textbook.
Studying just what is required by the syllabus will be enough.
Don't spend too much time studying other miscellaneous information given in the textbook.

If your goal is to just study for the exam: Find out what type of questions will be asked in the exam. Then divide your topics depending on their priority and weightage as per the examination point.

Try taking the help of the previous year's questions papers to get an idea. Once you know your end goal. You can plan out the time and energy you need to invest in the subject.
 Gather your study materials and always try to learn from the best source! Take the help of your teachers and friends when in need.

Know that every subject is different. Therefore each of them requires a different study strategy to learn THAT subject better.

You cannot use the same *smart techniques* which you use to study both history and science! These are different subjects hence, their study technique and approaches will be different.
It is possible, sometimes you may need to use more than 1 *smart technique* for a particular subject depending on the topics within the subject.

<u>**Key Points:**</u>
- *I'm reading math! Math is not to be read! It has to be practiced!*
- *The study strategy you use for maths can't be used to study history. And the Strategy used for history can't be used for science.*

- *Take your time to try and understand which **smart study techniques** given in this book can be used.*

6
Technique #1- Self Quizzing

#1 - Self Quizzing
This is an effective study technique that helps you to remember and recall the concepts better.
It also helps you to save time.
The golden rule of this technique is you read a topic.
Then you take a brief pause from time to time to ask yourself some thought-provoking questions without looking at the text.
While you ask yourself the questions, you also try to write down your answers.
This helps you to concentrate on the core idea of the topic.

→ When you pick a chapter or a topic, try dividing it into chunks. Which is dividing it into a paragraph or a page.

→ Next what you do is – study it once or twice.

→ Now without looking at the text, think about the types of questions you might ask on a quiz or test. Such as –
    ◆ 'What is the key context of the chapter/paragraph?'
    ◆ 'What are the important key points?'
    ◆ 'What is new to you?'
    ◆ 'What did you already know?'

→ Write down your answers.

→ Make sure to verify your answer in the end.

Writing the answers on your own, make you more confident. By verifying your answers, you can identify the strength and weaknesses of the topic.

This study technique comes very handily when you have a large portion to study. By dividing the topics into small chucks you avoid the stress of study.

Quizzing is an antidote for forgetfulness. Forgetting is human nature. By not testing yourself - you overestimate your ability.

Quizzing yourself while you study helps you identify your areas of strength and weakness within the topic.

It also gives you an overview of how much you actually know and how much you need to study.

Self Quizzing
Smart Study Technique

Topic

Your Topic

Q1 – What is the key context of the chapter/paragraph?

Your answer here, Key context of the selected topic.

Q2 – What are the important key points?

Your answer here – Important points of the selected topic

Q3 – What is new to you?

Your answer here – points which are new to you.

Q4 – What did you already know?

Your answer here – points which you already knew.

Q5 –   Any other questions to add

Q6 –   Any other questions to add

Any other questions to add

7
Technique #2 - Space repetition

Isn't it frustrating when you forget what you have studied?
When you're all prepared for an exam and then when you finally hit the revision, you realize that you have forgotten most of your study.
So, you end up studying it again.
Many students despite studying well are unable to recall what they've studied during the exams. They end up getting confused between concepts and begin to doubt everything.

So, Why can't we remember them?
Our memories can be tricky. We may be able to remember some random facts read years ago and yet immediately forget what we have just read mins ago.
It's because our memories are classified into short term and long term memories.

Whenever a new piece of information is received they are stored in short-term memory.
Short term memories get faded with time. Unless they are recalled occasionally.
When short-term memories are recalled they then turn into a long-term memory. These memories then are retained for a longer time.

Whenever a piece of information is received via our senses (eyes and ears) - If this information is not paid attention they are lost (no active learning).
But if given attention, they are stored into short term memory (i.e in case of active learning), but these memories are stored only for a short time. Hence the memories fade away.

In case the same memory is retrieved occasionally. If it is recalled again and again. This memory gets transferred into long-term memory and the information is stored for a longer time.

Think of your brain as a computer. When you put a file into a computer it gets processed and stored. But this computer has a unique way to operate.

It slowly erases fragments of data if that data isn't used. In case if you occasionally check those data, it recognizes as important and hence retains it.

This is similar to the way our memories work. To retain the information that we have studied should be recalled occasionally and repeatedly.

Here we use the **Spaced Repetition Technique**. This is the most powerful technique for improving your brain's ability to recall. This technique helps you to convert short term memory into long term memory.

Technique #2 - Spaced repetition:
Spaced repetition is all about introducing time intervals between study sessions. In essence, we study more than once but by leaving considerable time between study sessions.
We do that by scheduling a revision.

So basically when you're done studying a topic. Next, you plan out your time intervals for the revisions.

For example; you may study a topic today. You can schedule your 1st revision after 2 days.
Then the 2nd revision after 4 days from the 1st revision.
3rd after 8 days from 2nd revision and so on.
This way you can strengthen your memory and improve your ability to recall.

"Exercise in repeatedly recalling a thing strengthens the memory" Aristotle.

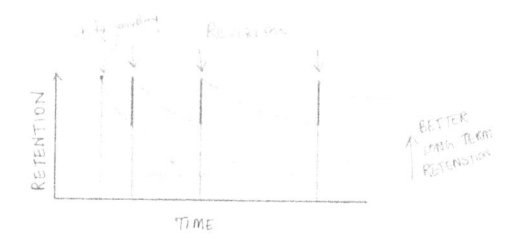

You must spread out your time intervals. If you don't leave enough time between your revision. It will be just another rote learning so space out your study to avoid mindless repetition.

This is the most powerful memory technique. This not only helps you retain your concepts longer in your memory. But also help you remember them clearly.

How to use this technique;
Step 1 - Study a topic.
Step 2 - Schedule your revision.
Step 3 - Quiz yourself after every scheduled revision.
Step 4 - Brush up the topics which you don't remember properly.

You could use your phone calendar reminders to remind you of your revision schedule. Also, make sure to evaluate your quiz answers by scoring yourself. You can use quiz questions from the previous technique.

Spaced Repetition
Smart Study Technique

Topic: _____ Date: _____ (date when you study)
Your Topic

Scheduling

Total No. of revision: _____ *Total number of revision you plan. It can be spread across 1 week or 3 months.*

Revision 1 : Time interval _____ On: _____ *On which day or time*

Revision 2 : Time interval _____ On: _____ *Time interval can be after hours or days or weeks*

Revision 3 : Time interval _____ On: _____

Revision 4 : Time interval _____ On: _____

Revision _ : Time interval _____ On: _____

Revision _ : Time interval _____ On: _____

Revision _ : Time interval _____ On: _____

Revision _ : Time interval _____ On: _____

Notes

....
....
....
....
....

eBook - How to Study Smart! NOT Hard!

8
Technique #8 - Random problem method

The Random Problem Method;

Mixing things up!

In this technique, you study more than one type of problem within a topic at a time.

For example; While studying physics formulas or maths study more than one type of problem at a time. This way you are alternating between different types of problems that require distinct solutions.

Quizzing yourself on various problem types, helps your brain to differentiate between concepts more thoroughly. Strengthens your memory association.

By mixing things up will make you constantly challenge your ability to recognize the problem type and choose the right answer.

Consider a cricket batsman- who practices batting by swinging at 20 fastballs, then 20 slower balls, and then 20 spin balls. This type of player will perform better in practice than the player who mixes it up.
However, the player who mixes things up by swinging at different pitches during training builds his ability to decipher and respond to each ball as it comes his way during the matches, thereby becoming a better batsman.

The result of the **Random Problem Method** improves your success in later tests where you must distinguish the kind of problem you're trying to solve to apply the accurate solution.

While you may feel this type of method is unproductive/ counterproductive or cause confusion between concepts. But, the opposite is true.

Studying more than one thing is to be encouraged to improve your learning potential.

So during exams, you don't get confused about which method to use when similar problems are asked.

Mixing problems not only help you figure out how to do a problem but also which strategies to use.
For example, in math. The major skill to solve a problem is to use the right procedure to solve the right problem. Many students perform poorly in math due to this reason. Because they get confused about similar problems and try to use a strategy that is not meant for that problem.
This technique helps you identify that. Interleaving helps you develop that skill. Instead of solving 10 multiplication problems, then 10 division problems than 10 additions. Mixing them up helps you identify the similarities and differences between the problem types.
It helps you review older concepts and develop the skills needed to choose the correct strategy for solving problems.

How to use:

- Pick a topic, for example, say a math problem. Identify how many types of problems or formulas are there.
- Next, you need to identify what makes them different and how.
    - What steps are similar
- Interchange the problems or formulas and solve them.
- Review your answers.

9
Technique #9 - SQ3R

SQ3R strategy

These days study materials are given in various formats.
Some are videos, audios, and most of the study materials are in written format.

Sometimes you have pages of information to read. It gets harder to read all of it. Understanding the material and staying focused gets more and more challenging if you don't know how to optimize what you read.

This method simplifies your reading time and helps you to study, understand, remember written information more quickly.

SQ3R stands for -Survey,

Question,
Read,
Recite, and
Review.

Step #S- Survey;
The first step:
You take a minute to go through the topic.
You try to pay attention to the structure of the topic such as layout, main points, heading, subheading, or other subtopics such as figures, tables, marginal information, and summary.
In general, you try to understand the main context of the given topic by NOT reading everything!
This usually takes a few mins.

Step #Q- Questions

Once you're done scanning.
Ask yourself questions about the topic.
Think of yourself as an examiner who is trying to make up a question paper. For example, try converting headings and subheadings into questions.
Next, you ask yourself more general questions such as,
- What is this chapter about?
- How does this information help me?
- What is this chapter trying to teach?
- What did I know already?

Draw a vertical line on the paper, write your questions on the left and later you can answer them on the right.

Step #R1 - Read

When you're done making up the questions.
Next step, you begin to read actively.
When you read you try to pay close attention to chapters, headings, and explanations. In this step, You read the topic in more detail instead of just skimming.

When required you can write down more questions as you read. While you also try to answer the previous questions.
Take your time to read more complicated topics.

The difference between passive and active read is that in passive reading is you barely read without engaging deep into the topic. Active reading is you pay attention and engage deep into the topic.

Step #R2 - Retrieve
This step is all about how you retrieve the information learned from your memory using your own words. You try to make a summary of the concept learned.
You can do this either orally or written whichever you feel comfortable with. One of the best ways to recall and make sure you understand the topic is to explain it to someone in the simple way possible.

Think of yourself as a teacher who is trying to teach a kid.

> Albert Einstein said, "If you can't explain it simply, you don't understand it well enough."

Albert Einstein used to explain his complex theory of relativity as,
*"When a man sits with a pretty girl for an hour, it seems like a minute. But let him sit on a **hot stove** for a minute—and it's longer than an hour. That's **relativity**."*

Step #R3 - Review
This will be the final step. Once you reach the end of the topic,
Read all the relevant parts again.
Go through your answers and verify them.
You are reviewing the material by repeating back to yourself what you have read using your own words.
SQ3R - Survey helps you prepare for study, therefore, effectively priming your brain.

SQ3R
Smart Study Technique

SQ3R - Survey - Questions - Read - Recite - Review

Topic: Your Topic

What is the Topic/Chapter all about?	
What is the key points of the topic?	
Notice any subtitles, heading or chapters. How are they framed?	
Describe a picture or graphics or diagram included in the topic.	
	Your Answers
Your Questions	

Notes

10
Technique #5 - Mnemonics

So far you have learned how to study the topic without rote learning, but there are certain facts that require memorization.

Facts such as names of planets, Spectrum of colors, Orders of mathematical operations, Trigonometric ratios. Sometimes these are easily memorized, sometimes they are not and the problem with easy memorization is that it is easily forgotten.

Also when it comes to even more complex facts to remember such as names of bones in a human skull, it becomes difficult to remember them.

One way to learn ANY fact is to use **Mnemonic devices.**

So, what are Mnemonic Devices?

Mnemonic Devices are Memory cues that help us remember certain facts or large amounts of information easily.
They can be made up into a song, or a rhyme. They are most commonly made up of an acronym or a phrase and also a sentence.

Mnemonics help us remember facts and are particularly useful when the order of things is important.
Imagine them being like your mental file cabinet. A place where you store the information, and you can retrieve them easily whenever you need them.

Let's look into some of the examples on how to can use a Mnemonic.
To remember the names of planets in order:

Mercury, Venus, Earth, Mars, Jupiter, Saturn, Uranus, Neptune, and Pluto.

For this, I can just remember,

My **V**ery **E**ducated **M**other **S**erved **U**s **N**ine **P**izzas

Do you notice the first letters of the words in the given sentence?
M - Mercury

V - Venus
E - Earth
M - Mars
J - Jupiter
S - Saturn
U - Uranus
N - Neptune
P - Pluto

Now, if you don't want to include pluto, you can remember:

My Very Educated Mother Served Us Nachos

More complex facts such as naming the bones in a human skull.
There are six bones in a skull:

Ethmoid, Temporal, Parietal, Occipital and frontal.

If you want to remember them from back to front.

Old People From Taxes Eat Spiders

The use of mnemonic devices improves learning efficiency. They help you remember faster, better, and help you retain them longer.

Example #1

Memorizing the Electromagnetic Spectrum in order of increasing frequency, you could use this acronym/sentence:

> *Raging Martians Invaded Venus Using X-ray Guns*

The order of increasing frequency of the electromagnetic spectrum is:
Radio,
Microwave,
Infrared,
Visible,
Ultraviolet,
X-rays, and
Gamma rays.

11
Motive to Study

The best way to get better at any subject is to approach it with a positive attitude. You can't expect to grow a watermelon if you have planted seeds of cucumber. In the same way, you can't expect a positive result with a negative attitude. You can't think about failing if you want to succeed.

If you wish to study a subject approach it with a good attitude, don't think how hard or how boring that subject is.

If you do think that way, it will be hard and tedious for you.

Don't take the opinion of your others for granted.

If they say this subject is challenging. Don't ever expect it will be the same for you. Try it out. Never make up your mind about the subject before trying. Maybe what others find challenging, you may find it easy.

Never Limit Yourself:

It's very often that students underestimate their abilities. Students with many potentials, who are capable of great things, limit themselves not by others but by their own beliefs.
"I can't do this."
"This is too much for me."
"I am not that smart."

> *It's often not their inabilities that stop people from achieving their goals. It's their Beliefs!*

They have a predefined notion that they will not achieve anything beyond that point!
So they never aim higher or even try to improve.
To stay motivated, aim a little higher than yesterday. Try to do a little more than yesterday. You don't have to do everything at once. Whatever you do, just do 1% better than yesterday. Each and everyone is capable of great things only if they could believe and work for it.
Have an affirmed belief that you can study any subject if you wish to.

Always aim for the Moon; if you miss, you will hit the Star.

12
One Last Thing

Always remember
Your grades don't define you!
Your weakness doesn't define you!
You are capable of great things, don't let anyone tell you otherwise.

I hope you found this book useful and try to use these techniques constructively. I don't expect you to use it all at once. Try to familiarise yourself with techniques. Experiment on different topics. Use this book as a reference.
If you found this book useful, I'd be grateful if you would post a quick review on Amazon.

Thank you so much for reading!

- Shahana S.
How to Study Smart! Not Hard!
Effective Scientifically proven
Smart Study Techniques to cut your study time in half!

Printed in Great Britain
by Amazon